START FISHING
A Guide for Beginn
Arnold Wiles

First published 1983 by Ernest Benn Limited
Sovereign Way, Tonbridge, Kent TN9 1RW

© Arnold Wiles 1983
Photographs and illustrations by Arnold Wiles
Colour Reproduction by Positive Colour, Maldon
Typesetting by Cold Composition Ltd, Tonbridge
Printed and bound in Spain by Grijelmo, S.A.

ISBN 0-510-00160-2

Ernest Benn
LONDON & TONBRIDGE

Basic Tackle:
The rod and reel

Choosing a rod

Today's rods are largely built of hollow glass fibre which combines lightness with strength. Rods made of a newer material called carbon fibre are even lighter and stronger, but they are somewhat more expensive and need not concern the novice angler to begin with. There is no one rod suitable for all kinds of fishing. Float fishing demands a long rod, a three-piece one about 11 ft. (3.3m) should be considered to begin with. A two-piece rod, 8-10 ft. (2.4-3.00m) long, is about right for light legering, and spinning even, and is a good second rod to consider. For ultra-light spinning a delicate 7 ft. (2.1m) rod comes into its own, as does the version with a cranked handle for use with a multiplier reel but, again, this type need not concern the beginner.

Choosing a reel

The reel should be chosen at the same time as the rod so that the two, when fixed together, feel balanced and comfortable in the hand.
The fixed spool reel is the most popular all-round reel in use. Your dealer will explain how to use it. Left and right-hand wind models are available. The closed-face reel is basically similar to a fixed spool reel but the spool is partly enclosed by a drum and it has advantages for competition fishing. The multiplier sits on top of the rod handle, since line is controlled by the thumb, but it is not easy to use in inexperienced hands.

A selection of reels: A centre-pin reel (top left) now little used, two fixed spool reels, a closed-face reel, a closed-face spinning reel and a multiplier.

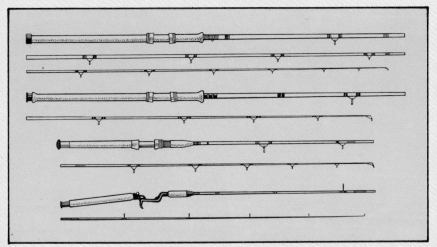

A basic selection of rods (above). A three-piece general-purpose float rod, a two-piece legering rod, and two two-piece light spinning rods, the lower with a cranked handle for multiplier reels only. This lad (right) seeks expert advice from an experienced tackle dealer when buying a first rod and reel.

How reels are fixed to rod handle

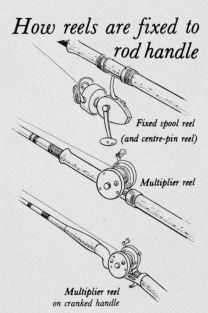

Fixed spool reel (and centre-pin reel)

Multiplier reel

Multiplier reel on cranked handle

Basic Tackle:
The line

Nylon monofilament (single strand) line is used almost exclusively by today's angler. It is a synthetic material, which is normally clear or occasionally tinted, and is almost invisible underwater.

Nylon lines are available on spools in various diameters and breaking strains, but a 4lb. (1.8kg) fish should not break a 4lb. breaking strain line as nylon has the ability to stretch and, of course, a rod acts as a shock absorber. Nylon can be difficult to tie so special knots have been developed for strength and reliability. Always look for a nice supple line when purchasing one, and make sure it comes from fresh stock. Age and exposure to light can weaken nylon and it can become frayed in use; so treat it carefully and renew it when necessary or you may lose the fish of a lifetime!

Nylon line is available on spools in various breaking strains and thicknesses. Spare reel spools (right) loaded with lines of different strengths.

Basic Tackle:

Floats

There is such a bewildering variety of floats that the beginner might well wonder what they can all be for. But don't worry; all floats serve the same basic purpose; to carry the bait at the desired depth in the water, and to indicate a bite by dipping, or disappearing from sight. They should be as light and sensitive as possible for the job in hand. Whilst a tiny, slender float might serve on a quiet stillwater pond, a larger, more robust float, which can be seen at 30 yards (27.4m) distance, might well be required for a fast-flowing river. The tops of floats are usually brightly coloured in red, orange or yellow for better visibility, whilst the underwater section is left dull to avoid alarming the fish. Floats are usually made of cork, balsa, or plastic, also from porcupine quills and the quills of large feathers.

You don't have to have a large number of floats like this to enjoy a day's fishing!

The indispensable net

Nets come in various sizes, with circular or triangular frames and, usually, detachable handles. Some have telescopic handles, and net frames which fold back for ease of carrying. Nets with the mesh of knotted cord have been much in use but are giving way to nets of much finer knotless mesh made from nylon. Be prepared for a big fish; buy the largest net you can afford.

Match the line to the fish: 2-4lb (0.9-1.8kg) line is suitable for a roach

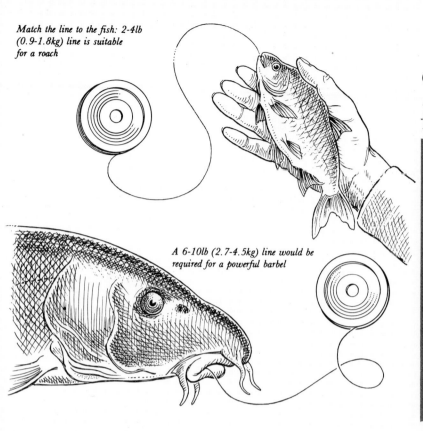

A 6-10lb (2.7-4.5kg) line would be required for a powerful barbel

Other useful items

Disgorgers, artery forceps and a pike gag (below left) useful for removing hooks. But see pike gag on page 22 (Right) a selection of rod rests.

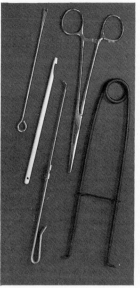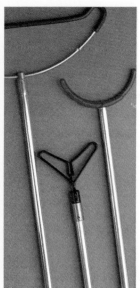

A variety of floats, each with a different purpose

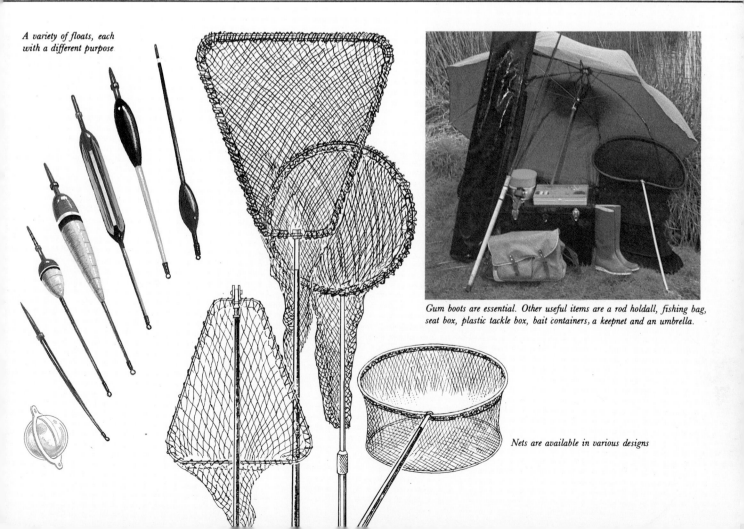

Gum boots are essential. Other useful items are a rod holdall, fishing bag, seat box, plastic tackle box, bait containers, a keepnet and an umbrella.

Nets are available in various designs

Basic tackle: Hooks, Weights, Swivels, Lures and Swimfeeders

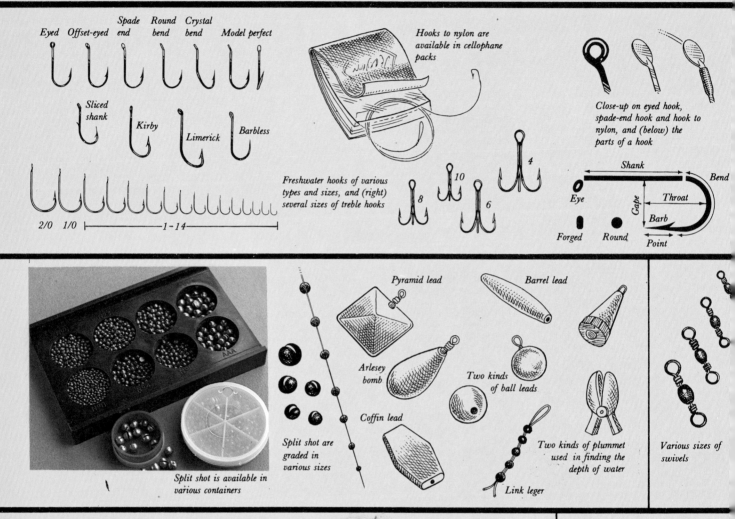

Eyed Offset-eyed Spade end Round bend Crystal bend Model perfect

Sliced shank Kirby Limerick Barbless

2/0 1/0 1-14

Hooks to nylon are available in cellophane packs

Freshwater hooks of various types and sizes, and (right) several sizes of treble hooks

8 10 6 4

Close-up on eyed hook, spade-end hook and hook to nylon, and (below) the parts of a hook

Shank Bend Eye Gape Throat Barb Forged Round Point

Split shot is available in various containers

Split shot are graded in various sizes

Pyramid lead Barrel lead

Arlesey bomb

Coffin lead

Two kinds of ball leads

Two kinds of plummet used in finding the depth of water

Link leger

Various sizes of swivels

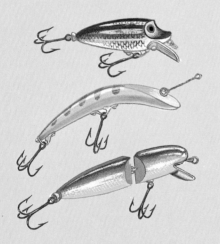

An assortment of plugs which float, dive and waggle

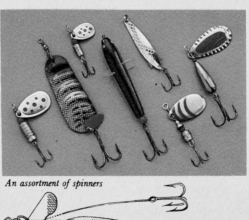

An assortment of spinners

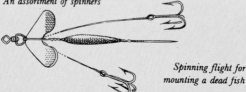

Spinning flight for mounting a dead fish

Spinners, Plugs

Spinners and plugs imitate small fish when you are fishing for predators such as perch and pike. Spinners do not imitate fish exactly. They are often coloured with stripes and spots, and are made of bright metal which flashes in water. Plugs are more accurate imitations of fish. They are buoyant and float, dive or waggle

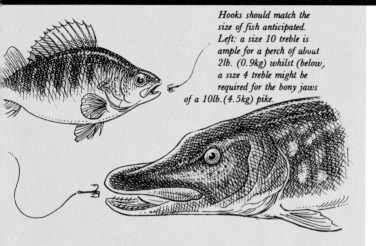

Hooks should match the size of fish anticipated. Left: a size 10 treble is ample for a perch of about 2lb. (0.9kg) whilst (below, a size 4 treble might be required for the bony jaws of a 10lb. (4.5kg) pike.

The right hook for the job

Hooks most commonly used in freshwater angling range in size from about nos. 6 to 20. Note that the smaller the hook, the larger is its number. Hooks with eyed shanks may be purchased loose and tied direct to the line, but the smallest sizes, used in catching the smaller fish, like roach and dace, are often made of fine wire with the end flattened like a spade. These are more difficult to tie to the very fine lines used. Many anglers prefer to buy them ready-tied in cellophane packs, as illustrated.

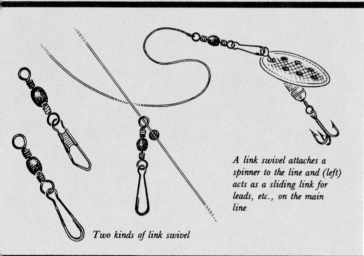

A link swivel attaches a spinner to the line and (left) acts as a sliding link for leads, etc., on the main line.

Two kinds of link swivel

Lead Weights and Swivels

Weights are made of lead. "Split shot", small balls of lead with a slit in the centre, can be pressed on to the line as required.
Larger weights are attached to the line by wire loops or by a hole through the centre. Some are flattened to hold bottom in strong currents, others are round or pear-shaped to roll on the bed of the stream with the current.
Swivels prevent line from twisting when drawing spinners through the water. Link swivels enable spinners and leads etc to be attached to, and removed from, the line at will.

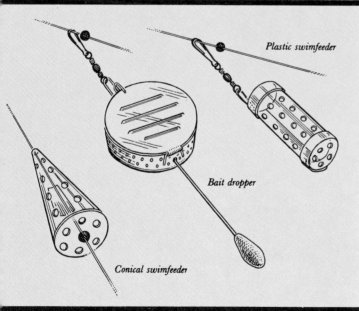

Plastic swimfeeder

Bait dropper

Conical swimfeeder

Swimfeeders and Baitdroppers

When fishing it is often desirable to groundbait with bread, maggots or other food items in a particular area. A swimfeeder is a plastic tube which is attached to the line by a link swivel. When packed with mashed bread or maggots, small holes all over the tube allow samples of the bait to drift free in the current.
The blockend feeder is packed with bait by removing a lid at the top. The open-ended feeder is packed with bait and closed at both ends with plugs of mashed bread. Baitdroppers are for carrying larger quantities of groundbait but are removed from the line when fishing.

Tackling up:

Assembling the rod and reel

With a 3-piece rod it is advisable to fix the finer, top section into the middle section first. Make sure the joints are firmly seated together, and sight through the rod rings to ensure they are all in line. Next slide the joined top sections firmly into the butt section and again ensure that the rings are all lined up. Now fix the reel to the rod handle by ensuring that the sliding rings, or in some cases a threaded ring on a special mount, are firmly tightened over the reel mounting. Fix the reel towards the top end of the handle so that it feels comfortable and ''balances'' the rod in your hand. Lastly, draw line from the reel (by adjusting the slipping clutch), and pass it through the rod rings taking care that none is missed out and that it is not twisted around the rod. Draw the line right back to the reel ready for fixing the float, weights and hook—collectively known as terminal tackle.

Assemble rod by first connecting the two top sections (top) and ensure that rings are in line (above) and that no ring is omitted when threading the line.

Some basic casting techniques

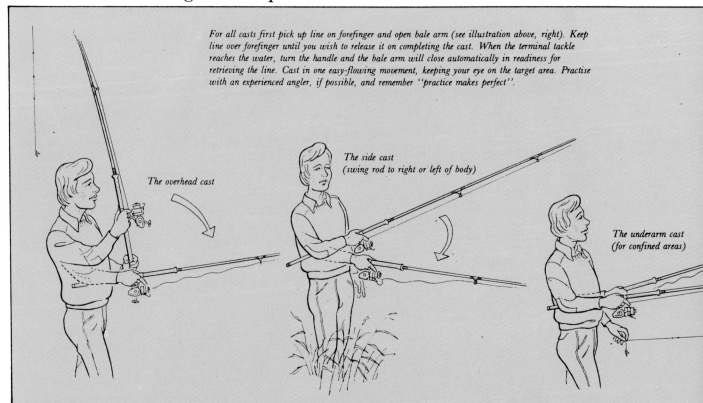

For all casts first pick up line on forefinger and open bale arm (see illustration above, right). Keep line over forefinger until you wish to release it on completing the cast. When the terminal tackle reaches the water, turn the handle and the bale arm will close automatically in readiness for retrieving the line. Cast in one easy-flowing movement, keeping your eye on the target area. Practise with an experienced angler, if possible, and remember ''practice makes perfect''.

The overhead cast

The side cast
(swing rod to right or left of body)

The underarm cast
(for confined areas)

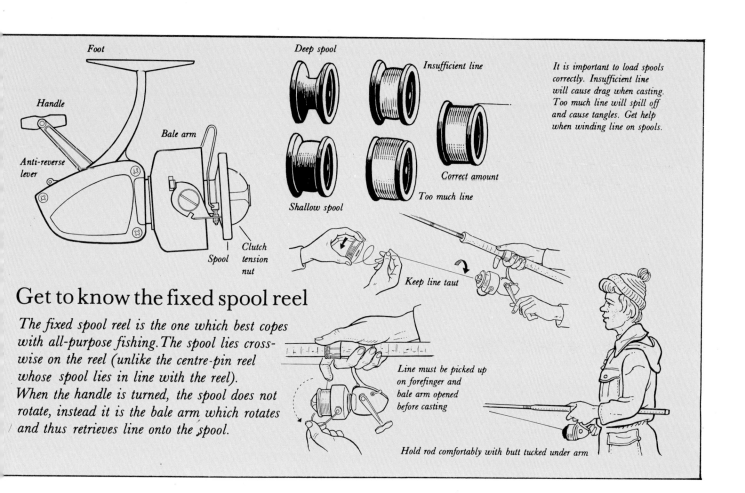

Foot

Handle

Anti-reverse lever

Bale arm

Spool

Clutch tension nut

Deep spool

Shallow spool

Insufficient line

Correct amount

Too much line

It is important to load spools correctly. Insufficient line will cause drag when casting. Too much line will spill off and cause tangles. Get help when winding line on spools.

Keep line taut

Line must be picked up on forefinger and bale arm opened before casting

Get to know the fixed spool reel

The fixed spool reel is the one which best copes with all-purpose fishing. The spool lies crosswise on the reel (unlike the centre-pin reel whose spool lies in line with the reel). When the handle is turned, the spool does not rotate, instead it is the bale arm which rotates and thus retrieves line onto the spool.

Hold rod comfortably with butt tucked under arm

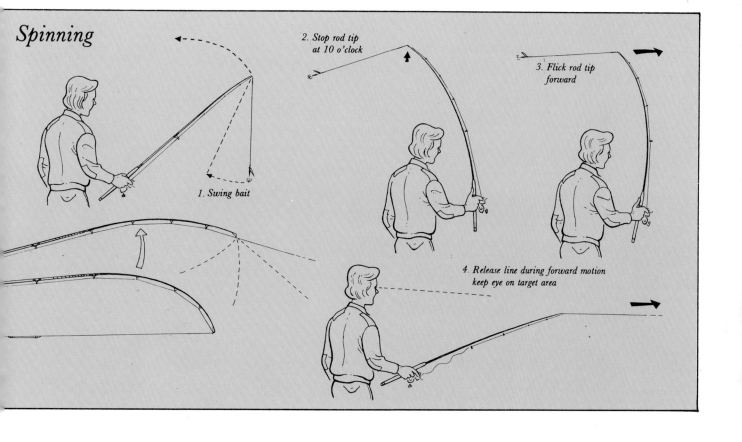

Spinning

2. Stop rod tip at 10 o'clock

3. Flick rod tip forward

1. Swing bait

4. Release line during forward motion keep eye on target area

Tackling up:

Float rigs and shotting

The correct combination of floats and the shot used to "cock" them is essential. A fish will soon reject a bait if it feels too much resistance from the float. The trick then is to use a float of sufficient weight to reach the required distance and then pinch enough shot on to ensure that only the tip of the float remains visible. Some floats have the amount of shot required to cock them marked on the stem i.e. 3AA; but you may have to find the correct amount by trial and error. Don't pinch the shot too tightly or you will bruise and weaken the line. Use pliers, not your teeth, if you don't want to spend good fishing time in the dentist's chair!

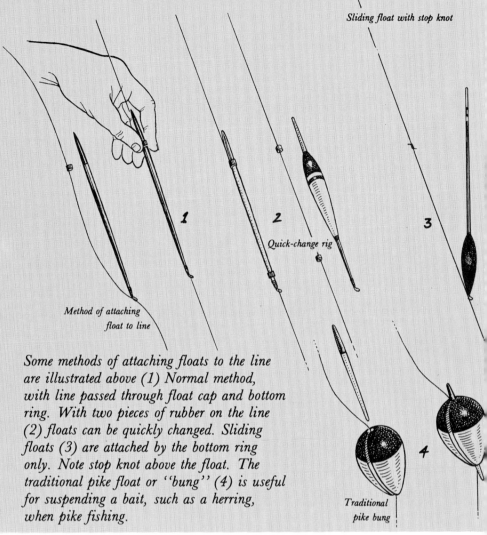

Sliding float with stop knot

Method of attaching float to line

Quick-change rig

Traditional pike bung

Some methods of attaching floats to the line are illustrated above (1) Normal method, with line passed through float cap and bottom ring. With two pieces of rubber on the line (2) floats can be quickly changed. Sliding floats (3) are attached by the bottom ring only. Note stop knot above the float. The traditional pike float or ''bung'' (4) is useful for suspending a bait, such as a herring, when pike fishing.

Float rigs to cope with various conditions

Special floats have been designed to cope with specific conditions and to carry varying amounts of shot and bait. Some have been designed to cast long distances or to hold course in turbulent water. Some have large cork bodies to support heavy baits or a long antenna for better visibility at long distances. Others are useful only for the most sensitive close-range fishing. Study the illustrations on the next page for some basic float rigs and shot patterns.

This lad trots the stream where two waters meet

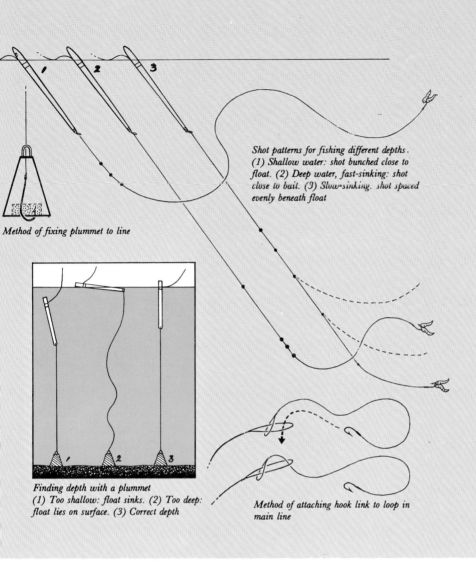

Method of fixing plummet to line

Finding depth with a plummet
(1) Too shallow: float sinks. (2) Too deep:
float lies on surface. (3) Correct depth

Shot patterns for fishing different depths.
(1) Shallow water: shot bunched close to
float. (2) Deep water, fast-sinking: shot
close to bait. (3) Slow-sinking. shot spaced
evenly beneath float

Method of attaching hook link to loop in
main line

Two nice chub and a barbel (top) and
(above) this successful young angler unhooks
a splendid 1lb. roach—the reward of
thoughtful angling.

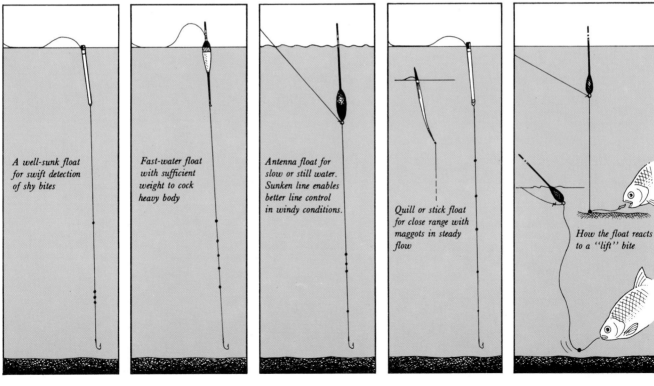

A well-sunk float for swift detection of shy bites

Fast-water float with sufficient weight to cock heavy body

Antenna float for slow or still water. Sunken line enables better line control in windy conditions.

Quill or stick float for close range with maggots in steady flow

How the float reacts to a "lift" bite

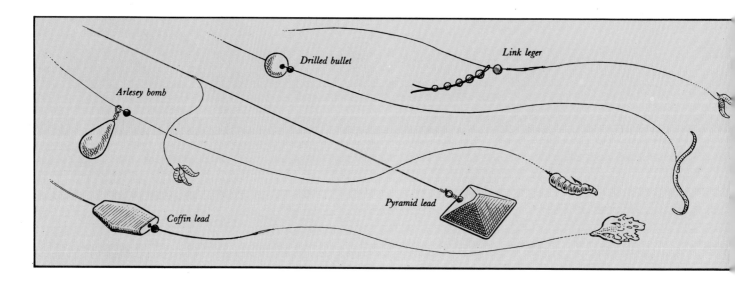

Tackling up:

Leger rigs and bite indicators

An alternative to float fishing is legering, a method by which the bait is held to the bed of river or lake in one precise spot or, in the case of streamy waters, allowed to roll from one spot to another by lifting the rod and letting the current take the weight, and the bait, to another chosen position.

With a drilled bullet on the line, baits can be cast into gravelly runs between weed beds in fast water so that the weight rolls in under the weeds

A combination of good tackle brings a fish to the net

and takes the bait to where the fish are likely to be lurking. An even more sensitive method, for smaller streams, perhaps, is the link leger; a few split shot nipped to a length of folded nylon, which is looped over the main line. Shot can be added or removed at will depending on the force of the current. Other leads, such as coffin and pyramid leads, are designed to lie hard on the bottom in strong currents and keep the bait firmly anchored in one place where a roving fish can find it. Note that the pyramid lead is specially designed to fish paternoster style, where the lead is attached to the bottom of the rig and the bait lies off the bottom on a separate length of line.

A bite indicator tip is an extra-slender addition to a rod which

Two kinds of bite indicator

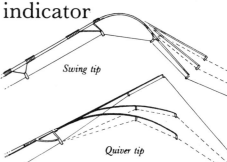

Swing tip

Quiver tip

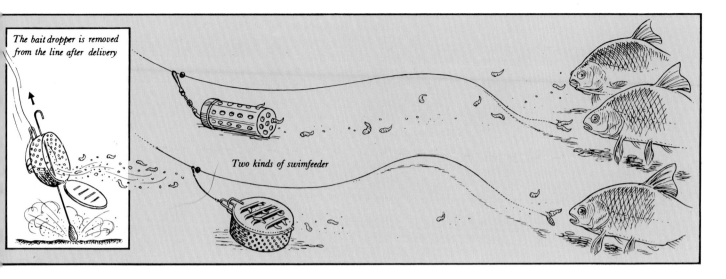

The bait dropper is removed from the line after delivery

Two kinds of swimfeeder

can be screwed to a specially-adapted top ring for use when legering. The most sensitive bite is recorded by the very fine tip, giving the angler early warning of when to strike. Illustrated below, left, are two popular models; but do-it-yourself bite indicators are easily made by pinching a small ball of dough or a piece of silver foil on the line, as illustrated. However, the most exciting way to detect bites is to hold the line between thumb and forefinger and you will actually be able to feel the bite. .

Swimfeeders and Baitdroppers

Anglers use swimfeeders and baitdroppers when they require samples of the hook bait to be placed in a particular spot. A strip of lead fixed in the tube keeps it in place on the river bed. The length of trail (distance between feeder and hook) can be varied to suit different conditions. A foot or two may be sufficient to allow the bait to swing enticingly in the current; the mashed bread, or

loose maggots, perhaps, washing from the feeder attract the fish to your baited hook. A longer trail, say 4ft. or 5ft. (1.2-1.5m), will help the current to wash your bait under the constantly-waving weed beds, whilst a very short trail of only 6″ (152mm) will bring the fish right up to your bait when the weather is cold and the fish may need tempting to feed.

Baitdroppers contain larger amounts of groundbait, or hookbait, but they are removed from the line after delivering the bait. They can also be used when fishing a sliding float in deep water.

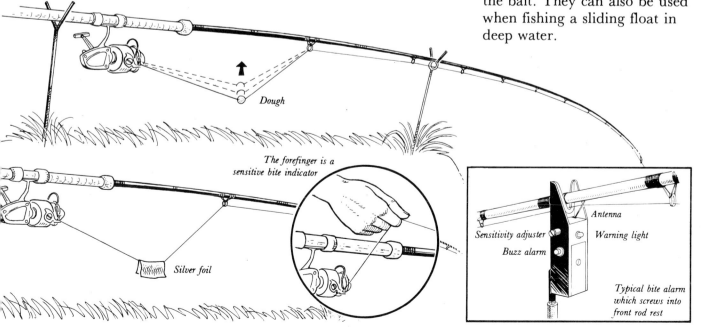

Dough

Silver foil

The forefinger is a sensitive bite indicator

Sensitivity adjuster
Buzz alarm
Antenna
Warning light

Typical bite alarm which screws into front rod rest

Tench

Grayling

Chub

Crucian Carp

Barbel

Dace

Know your fishes

Common Bream

Mirror Carp

Common Carp

Eel

Roach, rudd and bream are shoal fish found in both rivers and stillwaters. Dace and grayling also shoal, but they thrive only in moderately fast-flowing streams.

Mirror carp and leather (scaleless) carp are varieties of the common carp. The crucian carp is a much smaller species but has no barbels. All carp thrive in lakes, canals and slow-flowing rivers.

Barbel like deep, stony rivers with a moderately fast flow; chub prefer the slower-paced reaches and may also be found in some stillwaters. Tench inhabit well-weeded lakes and canals, as well as slow-flowing rivers.

Pike are equally at home in rivers, lakes and canals as are perch and the less-widely distributed zander. Eels are found in almost all waters and are well known for an ability to travel over land at night in wet conditions.

The wels (catfish) is one of our strangest-looking fish. Introduced into the Midlands from mainland Europe, it prefers thickly-weeded lakes with a muddy bottom.

Perch

Rudd

Roach

Pike

Zander

Wels or
Catfish

Arnold
Wiles

Some basic fishing methods

Check float so that current swings it to bank before retrieving

Swimming the stream

This is the basic method of float fishing so that one stretch or "swim" can be thoroughly fished. Groundbait, or a few samples of the hook bait, should be thrown in at frequent intervals upstream of the angler and swiftly followed by casting the float, also upstream, so that the baited hook follows behind the loose feed. As the float passes the angler it is necessary to "mend" the line by raising the rod and taking up slack line on the reel, but as the float passes below the angler the rod should be lowered and the bale arm of the reel disengaged to permit the line to be peeled off the spool by the free hand. The float must be allowed to travel as naturally as possible but contact must be maintained between float and rod tip so that a bite can be met with an immediate response.

At the end of the swim the rod tip should be raised to check the float. This will raise the bait in the water and often picks up a stray fish acting as "rearguard" in the shoal. Let the current swing your float to the bank before retrieving it or you will disturb your swim.

Long trotting

This is essentially the same as swimming the stream except that the angler fishes at much longer range. There may be a long clear swim to fish which cannot be exploited fully or approached in

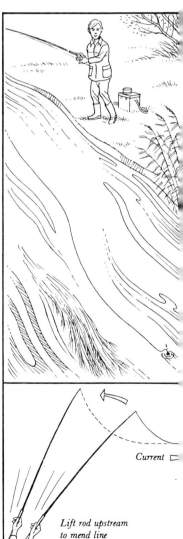

Current

Lift rod upstream to mend line

any other way due, perhaps, to a high or overgrown bank running its full length. Grayling and chub, for instance, are often found in long gravelly runs between weed beds, and only by positioning oneself at the top of the swim can the full length of it be fished.

The line must be allowed to peel off freely behind the float and a fixed spool reel can be used effectively with the bale arm left open, and if a slender, heavy-bodied float, preferably fluted to hold course in the current, is used to pull line off the spool. A longer rod of 12ft (3.7m) or so is an advantage as it gives greater float control and permits a long sweeping strike, essential for picking up line, and quick response to a bite at long range.

Legering

Basic rigs for legering—fishing hard on the bottom without a float—has been dealt with in some detail on page 12. It should be remembered that it does not have to be a static method. With a bag hung over your shoulder a water can be roamed at will; you can cast into all the likely-looking spots and move on as the fancy takes you. A pleasant

way to fish, especially when the weather is too cold for sitting about for long.

Laying-on, float legering, stret-pegging

Laying-on is a form of float fishing in which the weight is fixed on the line so that both weight and bait rest on the bottom. The distance between float and weight, (the weight should be the lightest possible), is set somewhat greater than the depth of the water. The float is half-cocked when the line is reeled tight, and bites are indicated by the float whether the line is tightened or falls slack. A substantial float, fixed top and bottom, is required for flowing water and a lightweight float, fixed only at the bottom, for stillwater.

Float legering differs only in that the line is free to run through the weight such as a drilled bullet or heavy link leger. This method is perhaps best suited to faster-flowing swims and to gain distance in stillwater.

Stret-pegging is a similar rig for flowing water, except that the weight is dislodged from the river bed from time to time by raising the rod and paying out line to

Float leger

Rolling leger

permit the weight to take up a new position a few yards further downstream. By this method a swim can be thoroughly searched without constantly retrieving and re-casting.

Stillwater tactics

Since there is no rush of water in stillwaters as in rivers, the pace of everything is quieter and slower. Fish do not have to intercept a bait quickly before it passes on the current; they can investigate a bait at leisure. It is necessary, therefore, to fish very quietly in stillwater. There may be many areas that cannot be covered (unless in a boat) and your efforts will be within casting range of the bank. Canal fishing (often at

close range) calls for extremely light lines and tiny slender floats, which react immediately to cautious bites. On the other hand, in some waters where tough lily stems and thick weeds are plentiful it will be necessary to clear swims of weed, and to scale up tackle for species such as tench and carp; both powerful fish which will soon make for cover when hooked.

Groundbait must be used sparingly since there is no current to wash it away. Because the beds of stillwaters are invariably muddy, it is often best to fish baits just clear of the bottom where they will be more easily seen. The "lift" method of float fishing is particularly suited to stillwaters (see page 11).

now that you have learned something of tackle and how to use it, let's go fishing for
CHUB

Chub are found in many of our rivers and streams, although not so frequently in stillwaters. In summer they can be sought in all but the fastest water, but in winter they undoubtedly prefer the quieter glides and slacks where they can search for food without expending too much energy. Immature chub may be found in shoals, as are roach and dace, but as they grow larger they break up into smaller groups, whilst larger specimens will become ''loners''. Trotting the stream with maggots is perhaps the best way to make contact with your first chub. Your tackle should not be too light where chub are concerned, and a reel loaded with 3-5lb. (1.36-2.27kg) line is about right. You will soon learn from watching other anglers where the likely swims are. A brightly coloured float might well scare the fish in very shallow water, in which case a bubble float should prove less alarming.

It is good fun to try pieces of floating crust, with samples thrown in from time to time to keep up the fishes' interest. It is possible to trot the stream with a floating bait. First remove float and weights and then grease the line to make it float. Grease incidentally can be bought in tackle shops and it can be useful when float fishing to keep the reel line on the surface, thus making it easier to keep in contact with the float. If using worms or paste they may have sufficient weight in themselves, so you might remove the float and try free lining.

In deeper swims you may have to use a larger, full-bodied float; one that will carry sufficient weight to get the bait quickly to the bottom, if necessary. Generally speaking, shoaling fish may be found in mid-water during the warmer months, whilst in winter they may be on or near the bottom. You should adjust the float from time to time until you find the depth at which the fish are feeding. Before long you may find that bites are coming from one particular spot, possibly where your groundbait is collecting in a depression in the river bed. Watch for this spot and be ready to strike. If no bites occur, check your float for a second or two at the end of the run; a bite may come as your bait rises enticingly in the water. It is quite likely by these methods that you will catch more roach or dace than chub, but the occasional chub will certainly take your bait, and a two-pounder will give you some idea of better things to come!

Much of the best chub fishing is done by cautiously stalking the bank and actually spotting them. Polarising glasses which cut out the glare and enable you to see through the water are invaluable. But chub are notoriously shy creatures; if they see you first they will take fright and simply melt into the nearest weed bed until danger is past. To get within casting distance you will have to move stealthily, wear drab clothing, and not flash your rod around like a wand. It pays to concentrate on known ''chubby'' spots, and cast to where they are actually seen to be lying.

Legering is the best method since it allows a bait to be accurately placed and to remain in position until, hopefully, a chub finds it. Obviously, it would not do to throw a leger weight exactly where

the chub are lying since the splash would be bound to send any self-respecting chub scurrying for shelter! But a rolling leger of just sufficient weight to hold bottom can be cast out and made to swing into position above the fish so that the bait, trailing 2ft. or 3ft. (0.6-0.9m) below, will come to rest not far from those capacious mouths. Alternatively, you can attach a swimfeeder to the line, particularly where the current may be washing away your loose groundbait too quickly.

In heavily weeded places it is best to cast upstream between the weed beds; this way a hooked fish, and your tackle, are less likely to be caught up in the weed since they are being pulled in the same direction as the weed growth.

A bite is indicated by the slackening of the line as the bait is picked up.

Whilst chub can prove difficult to tempt in bright sunshine and in heavily-fished waters, remember that they will often become bolder towards dusk, when they like to move in close to the banks. Concentration close under the bank in the last hour of daylight, may well provide a triumphant finish to the day.

Float-fished maggots (top) produced this fine 3lb 9oz (1.616kg) chub from the famous Throop waters of the Dorset Stour.

(Left and above) Safely ashore, the fortunate angler pauses to admire his catch.

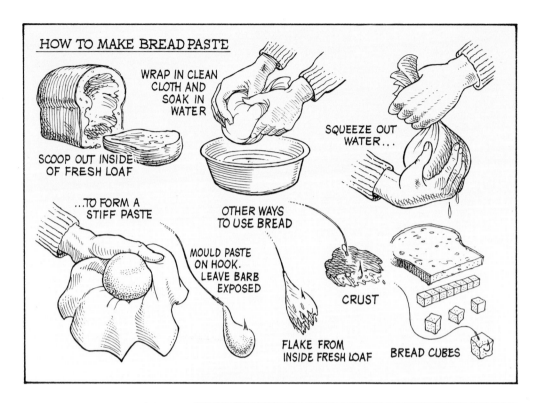

HOW TO MAKE BREAD PASTE

SCOOP OUT INSIDE OF FRESH LOAF

WRAP IN CLEAN CLOTH AND SOAK IN WATER

SQUEEZE OUT WATER...

...TO FORM A STIFF PASTE

MOULD PASTE ON HOOK. LEAVE BARB EXPOSED

OTHER WAYS TO USE BREAD

CRUST

FLAKE FROM INSIDE FRESH LOAF

BREAD CUBES

Baits: Preparation and use

Although bread in all forms, together with worms and maggots, are acceptable to many fish, there are many other baits which fish will take. Cheese paste, cubes of luncheon meat, fatty bacon and sausage and rusk, mixed to a paste, are all worth a try. Float-fished grains of sweetcorn, used singly or in bunches, stewed wheat and hempseed, fished on a size 14 hook, will take barbel, roach and dace. Groundbait is essential to attract fish to a "swim". Stale bread, soaked and mashed, is popular and various kinds of groundbait are available which produce a cloud of fine particles in the water. Small samples of the hook bait should be used with it

Maggots and Casters

Maggots, the most popular coarse fishing bait, can be bought in tackle shops by the pint measure, either white or dyed yellow, gold or pink. Keep cool in container (right). Maggots will turn to pupae, called "casters", (far right) They make good bait on fine hooks—but don't burst them.

Gather your own lobworms
You can always dig for worms, of course, but if you have a lawn, collecting them can be fun. After dark, when the ground is wet, lobworms come to the

surface; warm, humid evenings are best. Take a container and a shaded torch, and search the lawn carefully. Tread lightly; worms will retreat underground if they sense your presence. If you see a worm completely on the

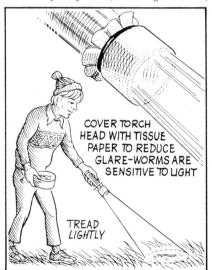

COVER TORCH HEAD WITH TISSUE PAPER TO REDUCE GLARE–WORMS ARE SENSITIVE TO LIGHT

TREAD LIGHTLY

GRASS MAY PARTLY CONCEAL WORM WHICH MAY STILL HAVE TAIL IN GROUND SO ALWAYS TRAP WORM IN MIDDLE FIRST...

...THEN TRAP AT EXIT HOLE TO PREVENT RETREAT. PULL GENTLY WITH FREE HAND UNTIL WORM 'GIVES IN'.

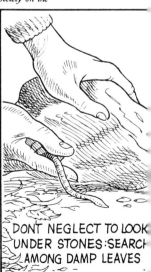

DON'T NEGLECT TO LOOK UNDER STONES : SEARCH AMONG DAMP LEAVES

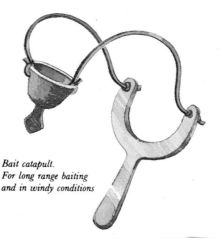

Bait catapult.
For long range baiting
and in windy conditions

Other baits

Hempseed, wheat, parboiled potatoes, peas and beans will all catch fish. If you are not afraid of creepy-crawlies, try woodlice, caterpillars, earwigs and other insects. Crayfish are good for chub; mussels, used whole or in pieces, will catch a variety of fish.

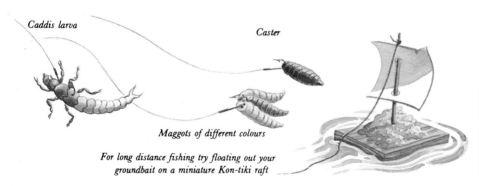

Caddis larva

Caster

Maggots of different colours

For long distance fishing try floating out your groundbait on a miniature Kon-tiki raft

surface, pick it up and pop it in your container. But if only part of the worm is visible, trap it first with a forefinger (see below) or it will "go to ground" at the merest touch.

With little effort you can make your own wormery to provide a ready supply of red worms and brandlings.

KEEP WORMS FOR IMMEDIATE USE IN DAMP MOSS MIXED WITH A LITTLE SAND TO SCOUR AND TOUGHEN THEM

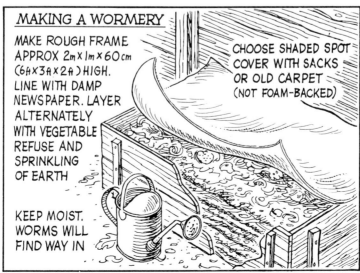

MAKING A WORMERY

MAKE ROUGH FRAME APPROX 2m×1m×60cm (6ft×3ft×2ft) HIGH. LINE WITH DAMP NEWSPAPER. LAYER ALTERNATELY WITH VEGETABLE REFUSE AND SPRINKLING OF EARTH

CHOOSE SHADED SPOT COVER WITH SACKS OR OLD CARPET (NOT FOAM-BACKED)

KEEP MOIST. WORMS WILL FIND WAY IN

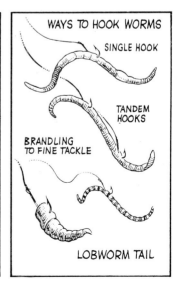

WAYS TO HOOK WORMS

SINGLE HOOK

TANDEM HOOKS

BRANDLING TO FINE TACKLE

LOBWORM TAIL

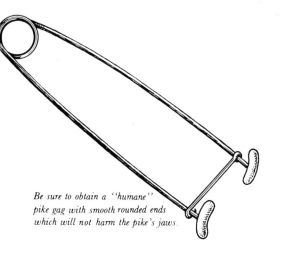

*Be sure to obtain a ''humane''
pike gag with smooth rounded ends
which will not harm the pike's jaws.*

there are thrills in store if you fish for that evil-eyed predator the **PIKE**

Of all freshwater fish the pike, perhaps, offers the best opportunity for the novice angler to catch a really large specimen. Other species grow to a good size, notably carp and barbel, but they are often very difficult to catch, particularly on hard-fished waters, and only the experienced angler is likely to bring them to net. Pike, however, whilst attaining considerable weights (the record stands at 47lb 11oz (21.63kg) are frequently caught in double-figure weights. Even a 5lb. (2.3kg) fish will look big to you and have you trembling at the knees before you have it, glistening-wet, on the bank. The trouble with this species is that it does not necessarily feed from day to day like other fish. After feeding ravenously for a day or so a pike may lie up quietly for some time, digesting its meal and thinking, no doubt, of its next meal to come!

Although built for speed, with its slender shape and large fins, the pike is really a lazy fish. Its speed is reserved for short, sharp bursts when it pounces on its unsuspecting prey from the cover of underwater vegetation, with which it is well camouflaged.

Tackle for pike should be on the robust side. A 10-11ft. (3.04-3.35m) hollow glass fibre rod, powerful enough to cast a 4oz. (0.113kg) bait and to strike into a heavy fish, together with a 10-15lb (4.54-6.8kg) line will cope with any pike and will serve also for spinning. However, a pike's sharp teeth can easily fray or cut your line so it is advisable to use a trace of 18″ (0.46m) or so of wire between the hooks and main line. This is simply a length of braided wire with a swivel at one end, for attaching to the main line, and a link swivel at the other end for attaching spinners, etc. Wire traces are available from tackle shops, and kits are available for making up your own more cheaply.

Despite the use of swivels, the line can become twisted and snarled by the spinning action of the lures. For extra weight a piece of folded sheet-lead or a washer folded over, should be fixed on the trace close to the top swivel; this also acts as a stabilizer which prevents twisting of the line. Another device is a vane of celluloid, threaded onto the trace which hangs down like a keel. Spinning with artificial lures is, in my opinion, the best method

for the novice pike angler to begin with. Nothing could be more simple than to carry a selection of spinners and plugs and to roam the banks casting into all the likely-looking spots that take your fancy; a gap between thick weed beds, perhaps, a run of clear water alongside a bed of rushes or a deep hole under the bank overhung by an alder tree. But remember that pike, being lethargic, prefer quiet backwaters, the mouths of side

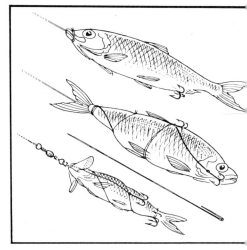

Two ways to mount a herring deadbait and a sprat on a spinning flight. A baiting needle can be made from a length of stout wire.

A fine 17lb. (7.71kg) pike safely in a suitably large net.

streams and deep sluggish holes away from the full force of the current. The trick with spinning is to spin slowly and erratically, varying the speed, direction and depth of the lure as it is retrieved. The idea is to suggest a sick or injured fish which will stimulate a pike into action.

An alternative to spinning is deadbaiting—a method of presenting a dead fish on the bottom, or suspended beneath a float, in quiet backwaters and eddies. Pike are scavengers who readily mop up dead or dying fish when on the feed. Freshly-killed roach or dace of 4-6oz (113-160gm) make excellent baits. When roach are scarce in a particular water avoid using them. Smaller species, like gudgeon or bleak, can be mounted on a large hook, two or three at a time.

These two pike (left) fell to herring deadbaits. This pike's jaws (above), are carefully examined and artery forceps are used to remove the hooks.

This young angler casts a sprat for pike in a small stream.

A hungry pike will not turn up its nose at such an unusual item on the menu!

The trouble with using freshly-killed bait is that they first have to be caught—and many an experienced angler has found it difficult to catch a few dace precisely when needed. Fortunately sea fish, such as herring and sprats, straight from the fishmonger or deep-freeze, also make excellent baits; their oily nature produces an enticing fishy aroma for the pike to home-in on. Pieces of fish thrown in around your bait will make appetizing titbits before the main meal. Deadbaits are usually fished head down on a wire trace armed with at least two treble hooks; one set in the angle of the jaw or gill slit, the other about mid-way down the flank.

The bait should be bound with fine wire or strong thread to keep the hooks securely in place, and tied in at the tail. No additional weight is necessary.

Whilst deadbaiting is something of a waiting game there is no need to remain static. Likely-looking places can be given half-an-hour or so with more time devoted to known "hot spots". When pike are not very active, it pays to stimulate their interest by moving the bait occasionally with a few turns of the reel handle.

A float can be used as a bite indicator, alternatively you can watch the line for a run. The rod should be propped in a rod rest, preferably two, with the bale arm of the reel left open so that the line (after a bobbin-type bite indicator has fallen off) can run freely.

Timing the strike when a pike picks up your deadbait is important. A pike takes a fish, dead or alive, crosswise in its

How to retrieve a small deadbait

When pike are on-feed it is not unusual to catch several in a day. (Below) pike should always be returned carefully to the water.

You must wait until the line is moving at a steady pace and the pike has taken off about five yards and then strike. Actuate the bale arm of the reel with a turn of the handle, wait for line to tighten, and strike the rod away from the run in a sweeping sideways direction and, with luck, the pike will be yours!

If deadbaiting is not active enough for you, you can keep yourself and your bait on the move by working it, head first, through the water as though it were a living fish. Sprats, being bright and silvery, make excellent baits. They are mounted by passing the trace from vent to mouth with a baiting needle. The bait is prevented from flying off the trace when casting by tying at the head with wire or thread. Another method of mounting a small deadbait is to use a spinning flight. This has an advantage in that the bait can be made to hang in the current more effectively, particularly in holes under the bank. However, a straight retrieve is not likely to prove very effective.

After casting the bait to a likely spot it should be allowed to sink for a few seconds. When you judge the bait to be near the bed, the rod tip should be raised and the reel handle turned to draw the bait forwards and back towards the surface, when the movement is repeated, as before. In this way the bait is made to rise and fall in an enticing manner. Again the speed of retrieve should be varied, and the rod

top jigged from side-to-side, to suggest the erratic movements of a sick or injured fish. Incidentally, you may hear fearful tales of the viciousness of pike and how they will bite your hand or even attack you. Make no mistake about it, pike are quite capable of swallowing a duckling or a water vole but, like most other wild creatures, they are afraid of man and soon make off at his approach. It has been recorded that a pike once grabbed a person's hand, which had a ring on one finger as it was dangled in the water from a slowly-moving boat. Apparently the pike mistook the flash of the ring and the movement of the hand for a small fish, or a water bird perhaps, and launched an attack. Such an unusual event, repeated and embellished-upon

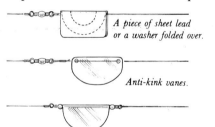

A piece of sheet lead or a washer folded over.

Anti-kink vanes.

over the years, soon grows into fanciful tales of monster pike swallowing people whole for breakfast!

To sum up then, a pike will not attack you, or attempt to bite you, in the water or on the bank but, because of its large powerful jaws filled with very sharp teeth (which are used to grip a fish not to chew it) you would be well advised to treat it with respect. Always use a spring gag to keep the pike's jaws open and always remove hooks with artery forceps for if the pike ''kicks'' whilst in your hands you may find to your cost that the pike, or the hooks, have caught *you*!

jaws, then turns its head first before swallowing it. When you see the bobbin move towards rod, indicating that a pike has taken your bait, you must resist the temptation to strike or you will almost certainly pull the bait from the pike's jaws without hooking it.

Spring

Rivers may be bank-high after February floods, and fish should be sought in quiet eddies and backwaters. Time now for the best of pike fishing; many a specimen pike has been caught at the "backend" of the season.

By March, all fish should be in prime condition, and ready for spawning as insect life becomes more plentiful providing increased food after the lean winter months. Sadly, 15th March sees the beginning of the close season when fish must be given a chance to breed unhindered. When the "glorious 16th" of June arrives, marking the beginning of a new season, fish will be foraging throughout the river anxious to build up lost strength, and you should seek them anywhere that the current is likely to bring food to hungry fish.

By midsummer, roach, chub and dace will be feeding freely among the weed beds, and barbel will be in the streamy runs over bright gravel. Rising temperatures and a prolonged drop in the water level will bring fish to the faster, well-oxygenated, water of weirpools.

As autumn approaches, fish may still be widely distributed but by late October falling leaves and rotting weeds will sour the water, and fish may go off feed and prove difficult to catch.

From November onwards following the first flood, the river will be scoured clean again, and as temperatures drop fish will be moving into deeper water, but when the river is fast and high they will again be seeking the quieter, more sheltered spots.

Autumn

Fishing through the seasons

Summer

Winter

Make the most of match fishing

Many anglers prefer to fish alone or in the company of friends; others, usually members of angling clubs, revel in the friendly rivalry of match fishing; they like to pit their wits against their friends or members of another club. Since rods, reels, radios and TV sets, as well as substantial cash prizes, are frequently offered to successful competitors, there is plenty of incentive to "have a go". Some top match fishermen earn considerable sums on the match fishing circuit, both home and abroad; but standards are high and competition fierce.

Match fishing calls for a high degree of skill and dedication. Tackle is refined to near perfection. Only top-quality baits are used and, prior to a competition, much time is spent in bait and tackle preparation.

Competitors draw lots for their individual "swims" indicated by pegs driven into the bank at regular intervals. A whistle marks the beginning and end of the match, and fish caught are retained in large keepnets to be weighed-in at the end of the day under the watchful eye of competitors and officials alike. The catch may well be a few large fish or, more likely, a large number of small fish.

Make no mistake, the quick way to skill and expertise in angling is to join a club and see how other, more experienced, anglers set about the task of winning a match in varied waters and conditions.

KNOW HOW ... to tie knots

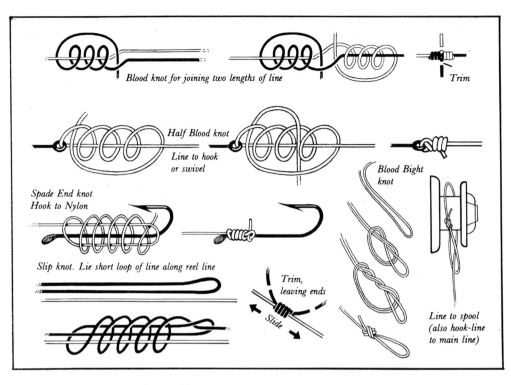

Blood knot for joining two lengths of line

Trim

Half Blood knot

Line to hook or swivel

Spade End knot Hook to Nylon

Blood Bight knot

Slip knot. Lie short loop of line along reel line

Trim, leaving ends

Slide

Line to spool (also hook-line to main line)

... to use a landing net

(1) Play fish out until it tires and lies on its side
(2) Sink net completely and draw fish over rim until enclosed by net frame
(3) Lift net upwards to enclose fish in bottom of net and draw to bank

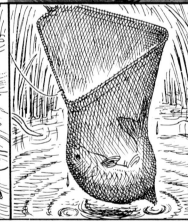

... to distinguish between roach and rudd, chub and dace

Roach and rudd can look alike but rudd have blood red fins and the dorsal fin is set further back. Chub and dace look similar when small but chub have convex dorsal and anal fins; dace fins are concave.

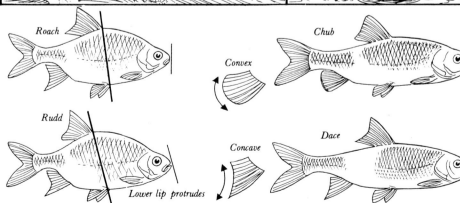

Roach

Rudd

Lower lip protrudes

Chub

Convex

Concave

Dace

. . . to remain inconspicuous

A fishless day may some-times be due to having scared the fish away in the first place. They are extremely sensitive to vibration, so a quiet approach is essential. Bright clothing can also scare fish from the banks so wear drab colours which blend with the background.

It is equally important to keep out of sight. Avoid high, open banks. Sit near the water level, behind bankside cover. Highly varnished rods can flash in sunshine so put a coat of matt varnish over the glossy varnish.

This lad fishes from an exposed groyne but he is well camouflaged and is sitting down. An experienced angler (top right) makes use of minimum available cover and wears green to remain inconspicuous.
These lads (bottom right) are too brightly dressed for such an exposed position.

. . . to describe a fish

It is useful to know the parts of a fish when discussing them with other anglers. Scales on fish vary in size from a few enormous ones, as on mirror carp, to the tiny scales of tench. All fish extract oxygen from the water through gills. Some have barbels (sense organs) on the mouth, and most have a lateral line which picks up vibrations in the water. Few freshwater fish have large teeth but watch out for those of pike and zander.

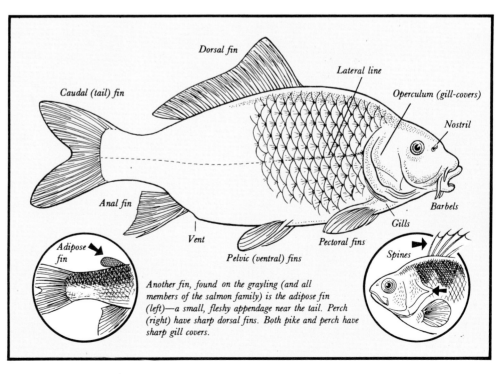

Another fin, found on the grayling (and all members of the salmon family) is the adipose fin (left)—a small, fleshy appendage near the tail. Perch (right) have sharp dorsal fins. Both pike and perch have sharp gill covers.

FISH EARLY-SEASON FOR THE LUSTY TENCH

Because it is commonly found in stillwater lakes, ponds, and sluggish canals, the tench is a good species for the novice angler to fish for. In the early season, from 16th June onwards, it can be a very obliging fish and not too difficult to catch; you can get to know your tackle, practice your casting, and generally get the feel of things without having to worry about, and allow for, the flow of water as in a river. You can sit yourself down in your chosen spot and study your float as it lies peacefully in the water (or your rod tip or bite indicator, if legering) and really *think* about what is going on underwater, and what best you can do with your tackle and your bait to bring a gleaming, golden-bronze tench into your net.

Tench are largely bottom-feeding fish who love nothing better than to root about in the mud around weed beds for blood worms and all kinds of insects. As they disturb the mud, air is released which rises to the surface in jets of fine bubbles—and very exciting it can be to see bubbles fizzing up in your swim announcing that tench have arrived and are nuzzling your groundbait.

Tench partly bury themselves in the mud and remain lethargic throughout the cold winter months, although they are occasionally caught on really mild days, so they are very much a summer fish. There is no doubt that early morning, at break of dawn, is the best time for tench so you will have to forsake your comfortable bed if you are to be at the waterside for the best of the action. Early in the season feeding is likely to continue throughout the day, with another marked increase in activity in late evening as dusk gathers into darkness. Within a few weeks the first feeding frenzy, after the long winter months of fasting, will subside; the tench will have become much more wary; many will have experienced the insides of landing nets

These lads are well on the way to making a useful bag of tench

and keepnets, and baits will be viewed with suspicion. The bold bites of the first weeks will give way to tentative, finicky ones. Now a tench will pick up a bait and, holding it lightly between rubbery lips, may circle around for a minute or so before deciding it is on to a good thing and finally accept it. Your float will be seen to bob and tremble and begin to wander aimlessly about the water's surface. This is the time for restraint and patience; only when the float disappears and slides underwater at a tangent should you lift your rod and strike—and even then you may miss your fish!

But first you should make preparations by clearing a "swim" (the area to fish in) and for this an old rake-

A helping hand with the net, and another nice tench to add to the total

sunrise and sunset are often the best times to catch tench—and it pays to fish early in the season before they get too smart for you!

Groundbait, in the form of well-mashed bread, bread crumbs, or sausage rusk bought from your tackle dealer, should be thrown into your swim to make a fine carpet of bait about 1 yd. (0.9m) in diameter; but when the tench arrive, remember the rule with all groundbaiting is "little and often". The object is to induce them to pick up titbits and, hopefully, your baited hook among them—not to stuff them with so much food that your hook bait may be overlooked! Samples of the hook bait, whether maggots, casters, or chopped worms should be thrown in with the groundbait. If you have time it pays to bait up a swim for a few days before actually fishing it. This gives the tench time to get accustomed to finding food regularly in one particular place so that when you start fishing you are likely to find them in a responsive mood.

In my experience, maggots and sweetcorn are the best all-round baits, whether float-fished or legered, and they can be most effective when legered with a swimfeeder.

head—better still, two tied back to back—attached to about 30 yds. (27.4m) of nylon cord is just the job; or you can drive some 6″ (152mm) nails into a length of heavy wood and attach the cord to a central cross-piece. You may have to tie on a piece of iron to make it sink. Throw the rake out as far as you can and rake a swim about 2 yds.

(1.8m) wide right up to the bank. Clear a space for yourself on the bank, if overgrown, making room for your net, rod rests and other tackle. Place your keepnet, if you have one, so that it lies horizontal in the water, giving plenty of space for any tench you catch. Don't let it hang vertically as this will confine your catch to the diameter of the net.

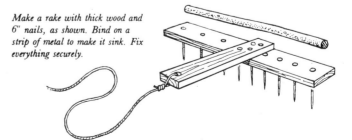

Make a rake with thick wood and 6″ nails, as shown. Bind on a strip of metal to make it sink. Fix everything securely.

A mid-water swim is raked clear of weed in preparation for a tench fishing session

A budding angler, having successfully netted a tench, learns how to unhook it carefully, after first wetting the hands

Worms will also work well at times, but unless you have a good supply, baiting up with chopped worms is not easy to keep going for long. Bread in various forms, soft paste, crust cubes and flake, will prove effective at times. A couple of maggots on the hook point with a pinch of flake on the shank may revive jaded appetites, as may soft cheese or breadpaste dipped in honey! If freshwater mussels are present, give them a try, either whole or in small pieces, but be sure to include some pieces in the groundbait.

All kinds of floats may be used provided they are light and sensitive.

For close range, a simple quill float or slim antenna float will do. Try fishing the bait "on the drop" with most of the shot bunched near the float so that your bait falls slowly through the water. Sometimes the bait is preferred just off the bottom, at other times it may not bring results unless it is fished right on the bottom. If bites still don't come, try moving the bait occasionally a few inches at a time by turning the reel handle. Alternatively, try the "lift" method by using a peacock quill or the very lightest float and setting the float over depth with just a single

shot a few inches from the bait. Only the very tip of the float should be visible. Remember that with this method a bite is registered when the float rises or falls flat so don't expect it to go under in the usual way. Wind can be a problem on open waters in which case put on an antenna float fixed at the bottom only with a rubber float cap to keep the line underwater.

Tench may sometimes be seen to be browsing on the undersides of lily pads by the movement of the leaves. A good trick is to cast your bait and draw the line gently over the leaves so that the bait is hanging

over the edge of a leaf just an inch or two underwater. But be prepared to steer your fish well clear of the lily pads, once hooked!

Lines should not be too heavy, although it should be remembered that thick weed beds and tough stems of water lilies are never far from a good tench swim. In open swims with bright clear water a 4lb. (1.8kg) line will be ample, but if space is restricted, with weeds close by, you will be unwise to use a line of less than 6lb. (2.7kg) breaking strain as, once hooked, your tench will surely dive for cover. Here you must apply side strain to turn your fish, having first ensured that your spool clutch is set with just enough "give" to avoid a break.

So give tench a try. You will be unlucky not to have landed two or three in the first few days—and the whole season will lie ahead of you!

Tactics for bait-shy tench